Have Heaven and Earth Passed Away?

A Study of Matthew 5:17-18
and the Passing of the Law of Moses

Have Heaven and Earth Passed Away?

A Study of Matthew 5:17-18
and the Passing of the Law of Moses

Don K. Preston (D. Div.)

JaDon Management Inc.
1405 4th Ave. N. W.
#109
Ardmore, OK. 73401
dkpret@cableone.net

ISBN: 978-1-937501-13-6

Logo Design: Joseph Vincent

Cover Design by:
Jeffrey T. McCormack
The Pendragon: Web & Graphic Design

If you wish to study more on the issues covered in this book we urge you to purchase some of the works listed in this work, and send for a listing of other works available. Be sure to visit our web-sites:

www.eschatology.org,
or
www.bibleprophecy.com.

HAVE HEAVEN AND EARTH PASSED AWAY?

Question: Have heaven and earth *passed* away? Ridiculous you say? Let me ask another question: Do you believe the Old Covenant has been done away? I dare say you will say it has. Few believers in Jesus would deny that he has established his New Covenant. *Well, if you believe the Old Covenant has passed away then you must believe that "heaven and earth" have passed away.* Please read the words of Jesus:

> "Think not that I am come to destroy the Law and the Prophets; I am not come to destroy, but to fulfill. Verily I say unto you, until heaven and earth pass, not one jot or one tittle shall pass from the law until all be fulfilled" (Matthew 5:17-18).

This book will answer a few questions about these verses. First, what did Jesus say had to happen before the law could pass away? Second, does the Bible tell us when these requirements would be met? Let us answer the first question.

UNTIL HEAVEN AND EARTH PASSES

Did you notice that Jesus said heaven and earth had to pass away *before the law could pass*? *At the very least*, the passing of "heaven and earth," and the fulfillment of every jot and every tittle of Torah are synchronous. Yes, he really did say it. Please, get your Bible right now, and read it for yourself! It has been my experience that a *lot of people* have never seen those words before. A relative of mine read the verse five times before admitting it actually says this.

Has the heaven and earth passed away? Well, obviously, physical heaven and earth haven't been destroyed. But read the text again, will you? Jesus *did* say *until heaven and earth pass away* the Old Law could not pass. Our choices here are limited.

If we understand the "heaven and earth" as physical heaven and earth then this means the Old Law is still in effect. If heaven and earth had to pass before the Old Law could pass, and if heaven and earth refers to physical heaven and earth, then, since physical heaven and earth still exist (have not passed), it must be true that the Old Law has not passed.

A person could say the Law here is the Law of Jesus, but this will not work because Jesus had not yet died to confirm his New Covenant. He was living under the Old Law at the time also. The Jews standing there were not concerned with the passing of Jesus' law. They were concerned with the Old Law. Finally, if this is speaking about the passing of Christ's law it contradicts the verses in the New Testament that teach that Jesus' word will never pass away (Matthew 24:35).

On the other hand, if we understand the "heaven and earth" here as a *metaphorical* "heaven and earth," then it puts this in a totally different light. Let us explore the definition of the heaven and earth.

DEFINING HEAVEN AND EARTH

Sadly many Bible students are unfamiliar with the apocalyptic and figurative language of the Bible. So many people like to say, "The Bible says what it means and means what it says." They seem to be saying there is no such thing as figurative or spiritual language. This is sad because a *lot* of the Bible is symbolic language. The term heaven and earth is a good example. (We are not saying the term heaven and earth never refers to material creation. We are saying this term is very often used figuratively).

Remember, Jesus was a Jew. As such he was raised hearing the Old Testament prophets taught in the synagogues. These prophets utilized highly metaphoric language. As the prophet of and to Israel (Matthew 15), Jesus was not only familiar with the language of the prophets, he used that language. So, the question is, how did the prophets use the term heaven and earth?

One thing that is significant is that the Old Testament prophets said "heaven and earth" had passed away lots of times. That strikes our modern mind as a bit strange, so let me give some examples of what I mean.

In Isaiah 13, Jehovah foretold the destruction of the grand city Babylon (v. 1). The prophecy was fulfilled initially within 15 years when the Assyrians sacked and pillaged the city. But here is the deal. In verse 10-13, Isaiah said that in that destruction, "The stars of heaven and their constellations shall not give their lights. The sun will be darkened in its going forth, and the moon will not cause its light to shine...Therefore, I will shake the heavens and the earth will move out of its place in the wrath of the Lord of Hosts."

Isaiah used hyperbolic, metaphoric language to describe the fall of Babylon. The *world* of the Babylonians came crashing down around their ears. Their "heaven and earth" was destroyed, because their capital city, the center of their world, fell. I think it is pretty clear that literal, physical heaven and earth was not destroyed when Babylon fell, right?

Another example is Isaiah 34. The language is graphic. It describes the dissolution of "heaven and earth" along with all the constellations. However, it is a prediction of the fall of the Edomite kingdom. Years later, Jeremiah (Jeremiah 25), Ezekiel (Ezekiel 35) and the book of Obadiah all reiterated the prediction of Edom's fall, using the same language. It sounded like the destruction of "heaven and earth," and it *was*, but it was not the end of physical creation. It was the end of *the world of Edom*. Edom fell to the Babylonians in B. C. 583 just a few short years after the Chaldeans had destroyed Jerusalem in B. C. 586. The book of Malachi actually looks back on the destruction of Edom as a historical fact (Malachi 1:2).

So, in each of these cases, and there are many others, "heaven and earth" was destroyed. But again, it is clear that the "heaven and earth" in view was the world, the society and the culture of the kingdom that was destroyed. Their *world, the political, cultural, social, theological world,* was destroyed, so, their "heaven and earth" was destroyed. And, the Old Testament predicted that the time was coming when Israel's "heaven and earth" would perish as well.

The prophet Isaiah predicted the passing of heaven and earth in chapter 24. He said the earth would be "utterly broken down, clean dissolved and completely removed" (v. 19). Now this sounds like the destruction of material creation, but closer examination reveals it to be speaking of the destruction of Israel's Covenant world under the imagery of "heaven and earth." Note that verse 5 gives the reason for the destruction, "they have broken the everlasting covenant." What covenant was that? It was *the Mosaic Covenant!* The Mosaic Covenant was the "everlasting covenant" of "the city of confusion," i.e. Jerusalem, mentioned in verse 10.

God would destroy "heaven and earth*" because Israel had broken her covenant with Jehovah.* Will the universe be destroyed because Israel will break the *Mosaic Covenant?* Wouldn't that demand that at some point the Mosaic Law would have to be restored? I am unaware of *any* school of interpretation that teaches that one day God will destroy the literal creation because of Israel's violation of *the Mosaic Covenant.* God will never destroy the literal "heaven and earth" because of Israel's violation of the Mosaic Covenant. But, Isaiah 24 speaks of the destruction of "heaven and earth" because of Israel's violation of the Mosaic Covenant. It is clear therefore, that the "heaven and earth" that God would destroy because of Israel's rebellion had to be a metaphoric "heaven and earth."

A dilemma is created for the literal interpretation of the text when we come to verse 22. In these verses God is depicted as dwelling gloriously in Mount Zion, that is, in Jerusalem, after the destruction of heaven and earth. If the earth has been destroyed how could literal Mount Zion still exist? The best explanation is to see that Isaiah was predicting the destruction of Israel's *covenant* heaven and earth because she had violated the Mosaic Covenant with Jehovah. As a result God's righteousness would remain in a New Zion – in a new *covenant* heaven and earth.

It is important to see that in Hebrews 12:18f, the inspired writer affirms that the Old Covenant "heaven and earth" delivered at Sinai was on the verge of being removed. Also, he said his audience had come to "Zion," and that they were in the process of receiving the kingdom that can never be moved (12:26-28). Thus, just as Isaiah foretold that Old Covenant Israel's heaven and earth would be destroyed, and that God would dwell in Zion, Hebrews depicts the removal of the "heaven and earth" of Old Covenant Israel and God dwelling in New Covenant Zion forever. Patently, for the writer of Hebrews, the removal of "heaven and earth" did not involve the dissolution of material creation. It involved the passing of the Old Covenant world of Israel.

Another example of "heaven and earth" being referent to the Covenant world of Israel, and not literal creation is Isaiah 51:16.

> "I have put my word in your mouth and have covered you with the shadow of my hand, to establish the heavens, to found the earth, and to say to Zion, 'You are my people'" (NASV). (The *New International Version* incorrectly

5

translates this verse. Check several translations.)

What is the point? We have two choices here. The first choice honors the past tense rendition of the majority of the translations. In this scenario, YHVH God is speaking to *Israel* about the things He had done in the past. He says He gave them His law, the Mosaic Covenant, the same law Jesus is speaking about in Matthew 5:17-18, *to establish heaven and lay the foundation of the earth!* Clearly, Jehovah is not saying He gave the Mosaic Covenant to Israel to create literal heaven and earth. Material creation existed long before Israel was ever given the Mosaic Covenant.

So, honoring the past tense of the majority of translations renders the meaning of the verse that Jehovah gave His covenant with Israel to *create their world - a covenant world with Jehovah. He did not give Torah to create literal heaven and earth.* God created Israel's "heaven and earth" by giving them His Covenant. Now, if He then destroyed *that* Old Covenant heaven and earth and gave a *New Covenant*, would He not thereby be creating *a New Heavens and New Earth?* This is precisely the thought in the New Covenant scriptures.

The second scenario hinges around the word and the motif of *Zion*, a motif that is eschatologically significant, and suggests that these verses should be seen as prophetic past tenses. In other words, YHVH was promising that in the last days, He would put His word in the heart of His new people and thereby establish "heaven and earth" and Zion.

The prophetic past tense actually makes better sense when we consider the *Zion* motif. After all, YHVH did not give the Law at Sinai to establish literal, national Zion, since Zion—the literal city of Jerusalem—was not established at Sinai. That would not come for many, many years. (It could be argued, however, that YHVH was referring to the people of Israel as Zion. Notice the language "to say to Zion, you are My people." Zion *was* the people!)

In either scenario, what cannot be missed is that the "heaven and earth" would be created through the giving of Covenant. The prophet was speaking of a covenantal heaven and earth–not a material globe with stars in the sky.

Notice that in Isaiah 51:6, YHVH foretold the destruction of "heaven and earth," with the righteousness of God remaining forever. This is the same "heaven and earth" he had established at Sinai. This is not a prediction of the passing of literal heaven and earth--it is a prediction of the passing of the old world of Israel so that the New Covenant world of Messiah would be established. The heaven and earth that Isaiah said would perish is the same heaven and earth Jesus said must pass before the Old Law would pass.

This lends itself to the second scenario above, in which YHVH anticipated the passing of the Old Covenant--"heaven and earth" but the promise to establish the New Covenant "heaven and earth." (Notice the direct parallel between Isaiah 51:5f and Matthew 24:35. I cannot develop it here, but, the parallels are powerful, and point to the destruction of the Temple, as heaven and earth, not the destruction of the literal, material creation). Old Israel's covenant was to pass away just as the New Covenant writers said (II Corinthians 3:10f; Hebrews 8:13; 12:25f).

The New Covenant of Christ was being given (Ephesians 3:3f; Hebrews 2:1f). Since the giving of Covenant created "heaven and earth," then the New Heaven and Earth of Christ would not be completed until the New Covenant was completely revealed. It therefore follows that if the New Heaven and Earth has not arrived *then Christ's New Covenant has not yet been fully revealed.* If Christ's New Covenant has been fully revealed then *the New Heavens and New Earth has fully come.*

Consider this carefully in light of 2 Peter 3 and Revelation 21-22, passages written as the process of revealing the New Covenant was yet incomplete. Both passages anticipated the arrival of the New Creation foretold by the Old Testament (i.e. Isaiah 65-66).

Isaiah 65-66 also predicted the passing of "heaven and earth," but as with the other prophecies noted above, it does not refer to the passing of physical creation. In chapter 65 God predicted several things:

1. Israel would fill the measure of her sin (v. 6-7): "Your sins and the sins of your fathers I will repay."

2. He would destroy them (v. 8-15): "The Lord God will slay you" (v.15).

3. Create a new people with a new name (v. 15-16): "The Lord God will slay you and call His servants by another name" (v. 15).

4. Create a New Heaven and Earth with a New Jerusalem (v. 17-19).

5. The creation of the New Heavens and Earth would follow the destruction of the Jews after they had filled the measure of their sins and been destroyed at the coming of the Lord in fire with his angels (Isaiah 66:15f). This is virtually ignored in the commentaries, but it is indisputably true. All one has to do is read the text.

6. The New Creation of Isaiah 65-66 is depicted as a time of *evangelism*, and Jew and Gentile being brought together under the banner of God (v. 19f).

Isaiah 65 said the New Creation would come when Israel had filled the measure of her sin and was destroyed. Do we have any clue as to when this was to happen?

In Matthew 23:31-39 Jesus said Israel would fill up the measure of her sin in his generation. In chapter 24 he predicted the passing of Israel's heaven and earth at his coming (v. 29-36). Now notice:

☞ Isaiah said Israel's old heaven and earth would not be destroyed until Israel had filled her sin,

☞ The new heaven and earth would not come until Israel's old heaven and earth was destroyed,

☞ Jesus said Israel would fill up the measure of her sin, and be destroyed at his coming in his generation,

☞Therefore, Israel's "heaven and earth" was destroyed at Jesus' coming against Israel, when the measure of her sin was full, in that generation.

In Matthew 24:2 Jesus predicted the destruction of the Temple in Jerusalem. This Temple was the very center of the Jewish world. This is where the genealogically confirmed Levitical priests offered sacrifices for sin. For Jesus to predict the utter desolation of that temple was the same as saying their world was about to come crashing down around their ears.

There are two major (false) assumptions made when commentators come to the questions that the disciples asked in response to Jesus' prediction.

The first assumption is that the disciples associated the destruction of the Temple with the end of the Christian age or the end of time. However ask yourself this question: *What age did the Temple symbolize?* Was it the Old Covenant age of

Moses or was it the New Covenant age? The answer is undeniable.

The *only age* associated with the Temple and Jerusalem was the Old Covenant age. To assume that the disciples linked the fall of Jerusalem with the end of the Christian age is disjunctive to say the very least. *Why would the disciples link the end of the Christian age with the fall of the Temple that represented the Mosaic age?*

In the first place, the Jews only believed in two ages. They believed in "this age" and the "age to come" (cf. Matthew 12:32). They believed that "this age" was the age of Moses and the Law, and that the "age to come" was the age of Messiah and the New Covenant (Hebrews 2:1-5). And, they believed that "this age" was to end, but that the age of Messiah would not end (Isaiah 9:6-9, 66:19f). To suggest that the disciples associated the fall of Jerusalem with the end of the Christian age contradicts what they believed and what Jesus taught. The only logical relationship between the fall of the Temple and the end of age is the correlation between the end of the age *represented by the Temple,* and this was the Mosaic age.

The second assumption that is made about the disciples' questions is based on the first. It is claimed that the disciples thought of the end of the material world when Jesus predicted the dissolution of the Temple, and that they were therefore confused or simply wrong; when they formulated their questions. However if it is true that the Temple represented the Mosaic Covenant age—and of course that is irrefutably true–then the disciples were not confused to link the destruction of the Temple with the end of that age.

So, the disciples *correctly* associated the destruction of the Temple with the end of the age, but it was the end of the Mosaic age, not the end of the Christian age. (See my book, *We Shall Meet Him in the Air, The Wedding of the King of kings,* for a full discussion of whether the disciples were confused or wrong when they posed their questions).

In graphic detail Jesus chronicled the events to occur before the fall of the Temple and the signs indicating its imminence (vs. 14-15). In highly apocalyptic (symbolic) language he described the fall itself:

> "The sun shall be darkened, and the moon shall not give its light, and the stars will fall from the sky, and the powers of the heaven shall be shaken, and then the sign of the Son of Man will appear in the sky, and then all the tribes of the earth will mourn, and they shall see the Son of Man coming in the clouds of the sky with power and great glory."

In verses 32-33 Jesus said that by heeding the signs they could know his coming was at hand. In verse 34 he assured them that generation would not pass away before all those things happened. In verse 35 Jesus reassured them that what he had said was true. He said, "Heaven and earth shall pass away, but my word shall never pass away."

It is important to understand that when Jesus said, "heaven and earth shall pass," that he was not referring to the literal creation. He had just left the Temple and was now predicting the destruction of that marvelous edifice. What is so often ignored, or unknown, is that the Jews of Jesus' day called the Temple "heaven and earth!"

Josephus, a Jewish historian of the first century, and a witness to the fall of Jerusalem in A.D. 70, describes the Temple in his work *The Antiquities of the Jews*. In his description of the Most Holy Place, and the Holy Place he says that the Most Holy Place "is, as it were, a Heaven, peculiar to God; but the space of the twenty cubits, (The Holy Place, DKP), is, as it were, sea

11

and land, on which men live."(Josephus, *Antiquities of the Jews*, Book 3, chapter 6:4, Unabridged, (Peabody, Mass, Hendrickson, 1987)87.

With this in mind, as we witness Jesus sitting on the Mount of Olives directly across from that Temple and predicting its destruction, we need to think like the Jews of the time. When discussing the destruction of the Temple, Jesus was discussing the destruction of "heaven and earth!" However he was not in any way predicting the destruction of the material universe. (It is becoming increasingly common for scholars to admit that the Jews never envisioned the end of time, or the destruction of material creation. Scholars such as Mark Nanos, N. T. Wright, R. T. France, Scott McKnight, etc. are all on record to this effect).

This verse is Jesus' way of contrasting the old world of Israel that was to perish, and his eternal new world. That old world would surely perish as he had just said═──but *his* world will never pass.

In verse 36 Jesus gave a final warning about knowing the time of those events. Although he informed them how to know when the event was near, and reassured them that it would definitely happen in that generation, he tells them they could not know the day and hour. They must therefore be watchful (v. 42f).

Can you see the relationship of Jesus' prediction of the passing of the "heaven and earth" in Matthew 24 with his statement in chapter 5:17-18? In chapter 24 he said their world, symbolized by the temple and city, was to pass away, and he expressed it in the imagery of the passing of heaven and earth. In chapter 5 he had already said the "heaven and earth" had to pass before the Law could pass.

As we have seen, Hebrews 12:25-28 speaks of the passing of the Old Covenant world under the imagery of the passing of heaven and earth. The writer alludes to the giving of the Law at Sinai, (remember Isaiah 51), as the shaking of earth. He says God promised to shake not only earth, but heaven also. This shaking signified removal, therefore God was promising to remove heaven and earth. Why? So that something that could not be removed would remain. Now notice: in verse 28 he says they *were at that time* receiving, (they had not already completely received it), a kingdom "that cannot be shaken." Now, if they were receiving an unshakable kingdom, this means the "heaven and earth" was being removed. Remember Jesus' words in Matthew 24:35. He said "heaven and earth" would pass, but his word would not pass. Jesus' world then, is unshakable. Hebrews is discussing the shaking of one world and the receiving of another unshakable kingdom. See the comparison?

Patently, physical heaven and earth was not being removed, but Hebrews was written just a few years before the fall of Jerusalem and the Temple, Israel's heaven and earth. Further, the Gospel had been preached for some time declaring the superiority of Christ and the imminent demise of the old world. The old world of Israel was on the verge of destruction. The new world was being delivered. Thus, we have another example of the Bible speaking of the passing of heaven and earth when it means the passing of the old world of Israel.

Space forbids full discussion of II Peter 3 and Revelation as further examples of scriptures speaking of the passing of heaven and earth when the meaning was the passing of the old world of Israel. However both Peter and John say the heaven and earth that was to perish was the same heaven and earth the Old Covenant had predicted to perish (II Peter 3:1-2; Revelation 22:6). 2 Peter 3 and Revelation anticipated the destruction of the Old Creation, and the coming of the New Creation that was foretold by the Old Testament prophets. In order for 2 Peter 3 and Revelation to be speaking of the destruction of literal creation, one must produce the Old Testament prophecies that foretold that event. However *there are no Old Testament prophecies of the destruction of literal creation!* The Old Testament prophecies of the destruction of "heaven and earth" in the last days, are predictions of the passing of the old world of Israel.

What have we seen then? We have seen that both the Old and New Covenant predicted the passing of "heaven and earth" when physical heaven and earth was not the subject. The world of Israel was the subject. This is what Jesus had in mind in Matthew 5:17-18, when he said, "until heaven and earth pass, not one jot or one tittle shall pass from the law." He was saying that until Israel's *world*, symbolized by the city and temple, was destroyed, the law would not pass away.

UNTIL ALL IS FULFILLED

Jesus not only said the Law would not pass until heaven and earth passed, he said the Law could not pass *until it was all fulfilled*. It is the unfortunate practice of many to essentially ignore the first *until* in Matthew 5:17-18. The Sabbatarians are most observant of the first *until*, insisting that since (physical) heaven and earth remains, the Law remains valid.

Dominionists likewise make the same argument claiming that since the literal creation remains in existence, the "Law of Moses" remains in effect (that is, some few parts of the Law remain in force, while the majority of it, the sacrifices and cultic observances, have passed). Of course, this violates Jesus' words. He said none would pass until it was all fulfilled. Both Sabbatarians and Dominionists say that some of the Law has passed, without even being fulfilled.

But, there are two *untils* of equal force in these verses. Jesus said when, and not until, *all* the Law was fulfilled the Law would pass. The Bible is emphatic in telling us when all the Law would be fulfilled, *and it is not at the end of time.*

In Daniel 9:24-27, Daniel was told that seventy weeks had been determined on his people and city, i.e. Jerusalem. By the end of this prophetic time period God promised that six things would be accomplished. Daniel was told that by the end of that period God would "seal up vision and prophecy." In my book *Seal Up Vision and Prophecy,* I show that, "seal up vision and prophecy" means the fulfillment of all prophecy.

Daniel's prophecy then, tells when all prophecy would be fulfilled. When would this be? The termination of Daniel's prophecy concerned *Israel and her capital city*, "Seventy weeks are determined on your people and on your holy city" (v. 24). There is not a word in Daniel 9 that pertains to the end of time or the end of the Christian age. The terminus of the seventy weeks, *when all prophecy would be fulfilled*, entailed the desolation of Jerusalem (v. 27).

Revelation confirms that all prophecy was to be fulfilled at the fall of Jerusalem. John was told that in the sounding of the seventh trumpet, "the mystery of God is finished, as He preached to His servants the prophets;" (Revelation 10:7). Thus, all prophecy would be fulfilled when the seventh trumpet would sound.

However the seventh trumpet and the Seventh Bowl of wrath correspond to one another, and the Seventh Bowl would be poured out on the city Babylon (Revelation 16). Many interpretations have been offered to identify this city, and yet the most obvious interpretation has been ignored. Revelation specifically identifies Babylon—it is the great city, "where our Lord was crucified" (11:8).

Jesus was not crucified in Rome, nor was he crucified "in" the Roman Catholic Church. He was not crucified "in" apostate Christianity. Jesus was crucified in Jerusalem! Our point is this, John predicted the fall of Babylon, the city where Jesus was crucified. He described this as the passing of heaven and earth (Revelation 18-21). He said all this was to "shortly take place." The time limitation on the fulfillment of John's prophecy precludes any application to the fall of Rome, the Catholic Church, the European Common Market, America, a restored literal Babylon, or any other entity. (See my *Who Is This Babylon?* book for vindication of this claim).

So, what we have in Revelation is perfect agreement with Daniel 9. Daniel said that all prophecy would be fulfilled by the end of the seventy weeks, and the terminus of that seventy weeks is the fall of Jerusalem in A.D. 70. John was told that all prophecy would be fulfilled in the judgment of Babylon, and Babylon of Revelation was none other than Old Covenant

16

Jerusalem. All prophecy was to be fulfilled in the judgment of A.D. 70.

We have Jesus' words as to when all prophecy was to be fulfilled, and they agree with Daniel and Revelation. In Luke 21:22 our Lord spoke of the destruction of Jerusalem, and said, "These be the days of vengeance in which all things that are written must be fulfilled." In verse 32 he emphatically said, "this generation will not pass away *until all things take place*" (my emphasis). Take note that Jesus said that "all things" would be fulfilled in his generation. While the word "all" can certainly be limited at times, there has to be strong, undeniable contextual reason for placing limits on that word. Jesus did not qualify his statement. It was simply "all things." That is a comprehensive term with incredible implications.

Verse 33 also contains Jesus' statement that, "heaven and earth shall pass away, but my words will by no means pass away." *Twice* we are told when all things would be fulfilled!

Here is the divine commentary on Daniel 9. Daniel was told that seventy weeks were determined on his holy city and the end of the seventy weeks would be a time of desolation (Daniel 9:27). At the end of the seventy weeks, all prophecy would be fulfilled. And now, in Luke, Jesus is speaking of the fall of Jerusalem, Daniel's "holy city," saying that when she would be desolated (Matthew 23:37-38), "all things that are written must be fulfilled." Such harmony cannot be ignored.

It is important to note that the millennialists agree that Luke 21:20-24 applies to the fall of Jerusalem in A.D. 70. This is destructive to their view, for Jesus *did say* that in those events, "These be the days of vengeance, when all things that are written must be fulfilled." Well, if *all things that are written* were fulfilled at that time, it is wrong to suggest that the *real* days of vengeance, e.g. the Great Tribulation, still lie in our future. Jesus *did not say* that the events of A.D. 70 were a foretaste of something greater, or the beginning of a sequence of events that would lead to the last days and the fulfillment of all prophecy. He said, "These be the days of vengeance, when all things that are written must be fulfilled."[1]

Luke 21 thus contains not only the fulfillment of Daniel 9, but the identical elements of Matthew 5:17-18, the passing of heaven and earth and the fulfillment of all prophecy, emphatically placed within the context of the destruction of Jerusalem in A.D. 70.

Note the perfect correlation of Daniel 9, Matthew 24, Revelation and Luke 21. They all tell of the time when all prophecy would be fulfilled. They all identify that time as the destruction of Jerusalem in A.D. 70.

In Matthew 5:17-18 Jesus said the Old Law would not pass away until all of it was fulfilled. Jesus said all that was written would be fulfilled when Jerusalem fell in his generation, therefore the Law did not pass until Jerusalem fell in Jesus' generation.

Jesus said "until heaven and earth pass" the Law would not pass. He also said, "until all be fulfilled," the Law would not pass. We have seen that the destruction of the Temple in A.D. 70 is spoken of as the passing of heaven and earth. We have also seen that Jesus said that was when all things that were written would be fulfilled. Since Israel's heaven and earth would pass when the Temple was destroyed, and since all things would be fulfilled when Jerusalem and the Temple was destroyed, we conclude that is the time when the Old Law would completely pass.

---

[1] See my *AD 70: A Shadow of the "Real End?"* For a full discussion of whether AD 70 foreshadowed the true end of the age, the end of the Christian age.

A LOOK AT HEBREWS 9:8-10

One of the key passages dealing with the passing of the Old Covenant is virtually ignored by many commentators. In Hebrews 9:8f, the inspired author tells us some very important things:

> "The Holy Spirit is signifying this, that the way into the Most Holy place has not yet been disclosed, while the outer tabernacle is still standing which is symbolic for the present time. Accordingly both gifts and sacrifices are offered which cannot make the worshiper perfect in conscience since they relate only to food and drink and various washings, regulations imposed until a time of reformation" (New American Standard).

Take special note of the *present tense* language. The writer is emphatic that the then present liturgy of the Temple and the priesthood was still "a symbol for the present time." That is *his* present time, not ours! Now, if the Law had passed away at the Cross, why did he not say, "It was a symbol of the things that have now been realized"? Why did he not tell them, as modern commentators do, that the Law was terminated at the Cross? Why did he say, so clearly, that the system was *divinely decreed* to remain valid, "until the time of reformation"?

Notice the correlation between Hebrews 9 and Matthew 5:17f. Jesus said none of the Old Covenant would pass until it was all fulfilled. In Hebrews, the writer tells us the Old Covenant system, *the sacrificial system* itself, was still valid when he wrote and would remain valid until that which was symbolized by its actions, was realized. One of the pressing questions is, What Old Covenant liturgical actions did he have in mind, when he said that the Old System would remain valid until what it symbolized was realized? He tells us in verse 12.

Now notice again that he says the Old System was symbolic and would stand until "the time of reformation."[2] The time of reformation was to be the time when what was *symbolized* was *realized*.[3] The Old Covenant would only pass when what it foretold and foreshadowed came to a reality. Verse 12 says, "But when Christ appeared as a high priest of the good things to come, (*about to come*, from *mello*), He entered through the greater and more perfect tabernacle, not made with hands, that is to say, not of this creation."

The *High Priestly actions of Christ* were the *anti-typical* fulfillment of the Old Covenant High Priestly *typical* actions. What does this mean? It means that until Jesus had fulfilled the prophetic actions of the Old Covenant High Priest, the Old Covenant could not pass. Remember, Hebrews 9 says that system was symbolic of better things to come, and was imposed until those things came, i.e. the time of reformation.

When did Jesus fulfill the High Priestly functions? In Hebrews 9:26 it says he appeared in the end of the age, and that has to be in the end of the Old Covenant age, to sacrifice himself. We have already seen that verse 11 says he, "appeared *as a high priest* of the good things about to (*mello*) come" So, Jesus appeared at the end of the Old Covenant age to fulfill the High Priestly actions.

In addition, just as the High Priest went into the Most Holy Place with the blood of the atonement sacrifice, Jesus entered the Most Holy Place (of heaven), "to appear in the presence of God for us" (v. 24). The author then says Jesus was about to "appear a second time, for salvation without reference to sin, to those who eagerly await Him." Christ's *Second Coming* would be the final action of His High Priestly Atonement function! It is vitally important to remember that the writer assured his

---

[2] See my *Like Father Like Son, On Clouds of Glory* for an in-depth study of the "time of reformation." This is a highly significant study.

audience, "Now in a very, very little while, the one who is coming will come, and will not tarry" (Hebrews 10:37).

So, Hebrews 9 tells us that the Old Covenant would stand until it reached its anticipated, prophetic goal, the time of reformation when Israel's hopes were realized. This would be when all of those typological feast days and ordinances would be fulfilled. That would be the *Second Coming*, when Jesus consummated the High Priestly function. This means that if the Old Covenant has been removed, the Second Coming has occurred, and conversely, *if the Second Coming has not occurred, then the Old Law remains valid.*

The Old Covenant System would remain valid until all that it foreshadowed and foretold was realized at the time of reformation (Hebrews 9:8-10). But, all that the Old Covenant foreshadowed and foretold was to be realized in the completion of Jesus' High Priestly functions, i.e. at his parousia (Hebrews 9:28). Therefore, the Old Covenant System would remain valid until the completion of Jesus' High Priestly functions, i.e. the *parousia*.

YES, BUT...OBJECTIONS CONSIDERED

T here are basically four objections to what we have just studied.

First, it is objected that the *end of the world* did not happen and Jesus did not come in the fall of Jerusalem.

Second, it is said that the Law could not pass at the destruction of Jerusalem because the Bible says it was nailed to the Cross.

Third, a corollary to number two, it is insisted that the Bible teaches that all the Old Law was fulfilled at the Cross.

Finally, many insist there is a difference between the "Law" that had to be fulfilled, and the Prophets. Let us begin with the first objection.

DID CHRIST COME IN A.D. 70?

To some this may seem a ridiculous question-but the Bible is emphatic that Jesus was to return in that first century generation before all of his disciples died. Jesus so stated in Matthew 16:27-28.

In no uncertain terms, Jesus, in this passage and many others, said he was to come in judgment in the first century generation. His predictions have troubled the church for centuries, and caused skeptics to assail the inspiration of scriptures. However when we understand the point of this book, that Jesus was never predicting his physical coming to put an end to human history, there is no problem. Jesus came, as promised, by means of the Romans, in the first century and terminated the Old Covenant world of Israel.

Matthew 24:29-31 speaks of him coming, with power and great glory to gather the saints. In verse 34 he said, "Verily I say to you, this generation will not pass, until all these things be fulfilled." He told Caiaphas he was coming in that generation (Matthew 26:64).

Please note that Jesus said, "Verily I say to you," (cf. Matthew 16:28, 24:34). This word "verily" means "Truly," and is the strongest assertion of the validity of what is said. If Jesus' promise, affirmed by the solemn, "Verily I say to you," failed, then he cannot be Lord. And, the fact is that the Bible affirms repeatedly that Christ's *parousia*, his second appearing if you please, was to occur in the first century.

The Hebrew writer said, "In a very little while, he that will come will come, and will not tarry" (10:37). James said, "The coming of the Lord has drawn near," and, "the judge stands right at the door" (James 5:7-9). He told his readers to be patient "until the coming of the Lord." Peter said, "the end of all things is at hand," and asserted Christ was, "ready to judge the living and the dead," when he wrote (I Peter 4:5,7). He even said, "the appointed time," for, "*the* judgment" had come (1 Peter 4:17).

Significantly, the Greek text of 1 Peter 4:17 uses the word *kairos* for *time*, and this means *appointed time*. Further, when Peter says it was the appointed time for judgment, he says it was the appointed time for "*the* judgment." The definite article is present. Thus, Peter affirms that the time God had appointed for the judgment (Acts 17:30-31) had arrived. This is an unequivocal statement about the nearness of the judgment in the first century, and cannot be dismissed.

In Revelation, the book begins with unequivocal affirmation of the nearness of the end (1:1-3) and at the end of the book Jesus said, "Behold, I come quickly" (22:12,10).

Someone will say that Jesus did not come back because time continues. This overlooks the very thing established earlier-- *the prophets did not predict the end of time*. They predicted the passing of the "heaven and earth" of Old Testament Israel. The end of time is not a Biblical subject. The Bible says the Christian age has *no end* (Ephesians 3:20-21).

Jesus said he was coming back in the generation that was living when he spoke. Are you willing to accept the word of the Lord of heaven or your own preconceived ideas about the end of the world? Just what does the authority of the Scriptures mean to you? What does *inspiration* mean?

DIDN'T THE LAW PASS AWAY AT THE CROSS?

T he second objection cited above says the Law could not have passed at the destruction of Jerusalem, because Paul says the Law was nailed to the Cross (Colossians 2:14f). In fact, *Paul said no such thing!*

First, note that Paul said it was *the sin debt*, and *the obligation to keep the Law* that was nailed to the Cross. Much could be said about this text, but space forbids it here. But please note that Paul is dealing with the *sin debt* being nailed to the Cross. He did not say that the Law itself was nailed to the Cross, and this is significant. The Law itself was still very much present, although fading away, when Hebrews was written, some time after Colossians (Hebrews 8:13). (See James D. G. Dunn, in *The New International Greek Testament Commentary*, (Grand Rapids, Paternoster, 1996)164+ for an exposition of the Greek text). Paul simply did not say the Law itself had been nailed to the Cross.

Second, many people confuse the *objective* passing of the Law with the *subjective* passing of the Law. Let me explain.

I once taught that Romans 7:1-7 said that Christ had put an end to the Law itself. That view is *absolutely fundamental* in amillennialism, my former tradition. In fact, if that tenet is false, the entire underpinning of much of Amillennialism is falsified. This is one reason why so many Amillennialists react so stridently and vehemently to the idea that Torah did not pass until AD 70.

If the law passed at the cross, Israel's last days were terminated at that point. However this violates Paul's very clear teaching in Romans 11, that God had not yet fulfilled all of His Old Covenant promises to Israel. Israel's eschaton, her last days, were not yet finished. Israel's last days were consummated with the fall of Jerusalem. See my book, *The Last Days*

Identified for a full discussion of the identity of the last days as the last days of Israel, and not the Christian dispensation.

The problem is that *Romans 7 says not one word about the Law passing away.* It says, "You have become dead to the Law, by the body of Christ," "but now, being delivered from the Law, having died to that which we were held by, so that we should serve in the newness of the Spirit, and not in the oldness of the Letter." (Romans 7:4,7). Now, is there a difference between the Law dying, *and a person dying to the Law*? That is like asking, is there a difference between you *personally* dying, or someone else dying? An illustration will help.

Remember the Berlin Wall? Before the collapse of that wall, thousands of people, desperate for freedom, risked their lives to get over, under, around, or through that wall. I remember vivid images of people who escaped and the joy they expressed. Okay, when they escaped, what happened to them (personally and *subjectively*) in regard to the law of East Berlin? The answer is that the person who made it over the wall to freedom *died to the law of Communism!* Was communism dead? No, at least not yet.

However I remember when the Berlin Wall came crumbling down followed by the demise of the Communist government. This was the *objective* demise of the Communist system itself. The ruling authorities were removed. Communism, *the Law itself,* then died.

Do you see the difference? Before Communism actually died in East Berlin, those who escaped that oppressive rule *died to the law.* However finally, that *system itself,* the objective system, then passed.

This is the way it was in the first century in regard to the Law. Those coming into Christ died (personally/ subjectively) to the obligation to keep the Law. It was "in the body of his flesh" and, "in him," that a person died to the Law (Cf. Romans 10:4; Ephesians 2:14f). When a person entered Christ through baptism they joined with his death. By joining Christ's death, they thereby died to the Law (Romans 6:3-10; 7:4-7). However the Law itself had not yet passed, (objectively) and would not pass until it was all fulfilled.

In 2 Corinthians 3, the apostle discusses the passing of the Old Covenant. In verse 11, he says, "If what is passing away (that is the Old Law, DKP) was glorious, what remains is much more glorious." (NKJV) Notice the *present tense* of the verse. This passage was written over 20 years after the Cross, yet Paul said the Old Law was passing, not *had* passed, away.

To drive this home even more see the next verse-but before that see Romans 8:24: "hope that is seen is no hope." Something realized is no longer anticipated—no longer the object of hope. Remember this as we go back to 2 Corinthians 3. In verse 12 Paul says, "Seeing then that we have such *hope*." What hope was that? Please go there *right now,* and see for yourself that it was the passing away of the Old Law. Paul, *twenty years after the death of Jesus on the Cross*, called the passing of the Old Law a *hope*! He *did not say*, "We had that hope, but it is now a reality." He said, "Seeing then that we have this hope." There is no way to escape the fact that Paul saw the passing of the Old Covenant as his hope.

But, not only was it his *hope*, that transformation from the Old Covenant to the New was *Paul's personal ministry*: "Therefore, since we have this ministry, as we have received mercy, we do not lose heart" (2 Corinthians 4:1). What ministry was he referring to? It was the ministry of the previous verse, the transition from the glory of the Old Covenant to the glory of the New.

Notice that Paul not only discussed the passing of the Law objectively, as his "hope," he also spoke of the subjective passing in the same context. In verse 16, he says, "When one turns to the Lord, the veil is taken away." In other words, just like in Romans and Ephesians, Paul said that when an individual turned to Christ, *they were freed from the Law*. Further, he said that the transition from the Old Covenant to the New was an on-going reality at that time, "we all...are being transformed into the same image from glory to glory." The contrast in glory is the contrast between the Old Covenant glory and the New Covenant glory. And Paul says that while individuals were dying to the Old Glory, as a *body*, i.e. "we all," they were *collectively* being transformed to the New Glory.

Finally, consider that in Hebrews 8:13, the writer emphatically says the Old Law was "growing old and is nigh unto vanishing away." This was written years after the Cross and yet affirms that the Law was still very much present, although now growing old and obsolete. It is important to see something here.

In my 2012 formal public debate with Joel McDurmon of American Vision, he argued that in Hebrews 8, the focus is not on the Mosaic *covenant* passing away, but rather, on the ceremonial and cultic practices that were about to "vanish away." This is specious. The grammatical focus and emphasis in the text is on the "covenant." This is demonstrated by the fact that the word covenant is used so many times, while the words needed to sustain McDurmon's view are totally missing. It is simply desperation to read "cultic practices" into the text, and to read "covenant" out of the text. (A book of that debate is available on my websites). Yet, McDurmon is not alone in his attempts to escape the force of Hebrews 8.

It is sometimes argued that the moment Jeremiah promised the New Covenant, the Old became "obsolete, ready to pass away." Thus, the Old Testament was supposedly old, obsolete and *ready to pass away* for almost 600 years—from Jeremiah to the Cross! There are several points that need to be made, but space will only allow a few.

1. Not one Old Testament writer after Jeremiah called the Old Testament "old," or "*ready* to pass away." If the OT was obsolete for nearly 600 years, don't you think the OT writers would have said so? In truth, it is the New Testament writers who first call the Old Covenant the "Old Testament" (2 Corinthians 3; Hebrews 8).

2. If the promise of a New Covenant instantly made the Old obsolete, then that principle means *Moses was obsolete as a prophet long before he ever died*! In Deuteronomy 18, Moses gave the promise of another prophet, to come after him. Did his ministry as Israel's prophet become obsolete the moment he gave that prediction? If the argument on Hebrews 8:13 is true, *then Moses was obsolete as a prophet* the moment he spoke of the coming of Christ, years before he passed from the scene.

3. If this view of Hebrews 8:13 is correct, the Old Testament was obsolete *before it was fully revealed*! This argument says the Old Testament was obsolete the moment Jeremiah promised the New Covenant. But the books of Daniel, Ezra, Nehemiah, Habakkuk, Haggai, Zechariah, and Malachi were all written *after Jeremiah's prediction*. Now, either these books are not part of the Old Testament, or they were obsolete the moment they were written.

4. If the promise of the end of the Old Covenant made it obsolete then the New Covenant was made obsolete *as soon as it was preached*. The logic (?) of the argument says that the moment a promise of something else is given, the present reality becomes obsolete. Well, the apostles (supposedly) predicted the end of the New Covenant age before it was fully revealed. We are told that Acts 3:19f predicts the final coming of the Lord at the end of the Christian age. But if the prediction of the end of something renders it immediately obsolete, then the Christian age was rendered obsolete in Acts 3—just a few days, (weeks at most) from Acts 2.

5. The *church* is the Temple of God (2 Corinthians 6:14-18; Ephesians 2:20f). But in Revelation 21 we find the prediction, written by John in approximately 64-68 A.D. of the coming of another Tabernacle of God-that is, it is *another* Tabernacle (according to the traditional views)! Thus, based upon the principle that the promise of something new immediately makes the first reality obsolete, the church became obsolete and ready to pass away the moment John wrote Revelation 21! The church became obsolete within 35 years after it was established and has been obsolete for nearly two thousand years.

These are just a few of the implications of saying the Old Covenant was made obsolete in Jeremiah's day instead of Jesus' generation. That view leads to doctrines that are palpably false and ridiculous. So, when someone says the Old Law was removed at the Cross this is a failure to honor the words of scripture. It fails to note the difference between individuals dying *to the Law*, and the passing of the Law itself.

ALL FULFILLED AT THE CROSS?

The he third objection says that on the Cross, Jesus fulfilled *all that was necessary for the passing of the Old Law,* i e. his sacrifice, and therefore, the Law could pass when his passion was completed. The verse offered as proof for this position is Luke 24:44—"These are the words I spoke to you while I was yet with you, that all things must be fulfilled which were written in the Law of Moses and the Prophets and the Psalms concerning me."

These words are construed by those who insist the Law fully passed at the Cross to mean that Jesus was saying his death was the fulfillment of all things necessary for the passing of the Law.

One thing that should immediately strike the reader is that Jesus is not even speaking of the passing of the law and the prerequisites for that. He *is* speaking of the necessity of the fulfillment of the law to be sure—but in contrast to those who appeal to this text, he is not saying, "now here is all that is necessary for the Old Covenant to pass away, I must suffer." In Matthew 5 Jesus is speaking of the prerequisites for the passing of the Law, and he says it must *all* be fulfilled. In Luke 24, Jesus was saying that his passion was part of the constituent elements of the Law that had to be fulfilled *not the only thing in the law that had to be fulfilled. Huge difference!*

Did Jesus limit "the fulfillment of all things" in Luke to his passion? Hardly! Go back to verse 27. Jesus taught his disciples: "And beginning at Moses and the prophets, he expounded to them in all the scriptures the things concerning himself." Notice the reference to all the scriptures.

Now read verse 26—"Ought not the Christ to have suffered these things *and to enter his glory*?" (Emphasis mine) In expounding the scriptures, and the need for him to fulfill *all things, Jesus did not stop at the Cross. He spoke of the glory to follow the Cross!*

Even those who believe the Law ended at Calvary do not believe Jesus entered his glory at the Cross. They place that at the Ascension or Pentecost. Jesus was expounding on the need to fulfill all things written in the Law and Prophets. He did not stop at the Cross but spoke of the glory to follow. It must be true therefore, that the fulfillment of all things written in the Law and Prophets included Christ's entrance into "glory." This was *after* the Cross, thus, the Law did not cease at the Cross.

These thoughts are corroborated in Acts 3:18f. In verse 18, Peter says Jesus fulfilled all things written concerning his suffering. But notice verses 21f. Peter tells them Christ would remain in *heaven until all things foretold by the prophets i.e. the restoration of all things, were fulfilled.* The restoration of all things is equivalent to the consummation of the glory of the Messiah. This is the time when Jesus would sit on the throne of his glory (Matthew 25:31f). Thus, Peter, in speaking of the restoration of all things was speaking of the fulfillment of the rest of the Old Covenant scriptures—and this fulfillment was directly related to the glory of Messiah. When we examine Luke 24, and see that Jesus said it was necessary for him to suffer and enter his glory, we can see it involves more than just the Cross. It involves the full establishment of the Kingdom of Messiah.

In addition, in Luke 24:44-47 Jesus said that not only must he suffer and enter his glory, but that, "remission and repentance of sins should be preached in all nations beginning at Jerusalem." The necessary fulfillment of all things *included world evangelism.* Patently this did not happen at the Cross—or Pentecost! Paul, writing in approximately A.D. 62, said the gospel had been preached into the entire world. But again, this certainly was not fulfilled at the Cross. Thus, since the completion of the World Mission was part of what Jesus said *had to be fulfilled*, it is improper to say that the Law passed before the Mission was fulfilled.

And consider: To say that all that was necessary to abrogate the Old Law was the Passion reverses Jesus' words in Matthew 5:17-18. Jesus said *none* of the law would pass until *all was fulfilled*. But the view that the Law passed at the Cross makes Jesus to say that *all* the Law would pass when *some* of it was fulfilled. Specifically, this objection has Jesus saying that *all the law would pass when one prediction, of his passion, was fulfilled*. But Jesus said all the Law and prophets had to be fulfilled, not just one prediction. When an interpretation completely reverses Christ's words, there is something wrong! Jesus not only said he had to suffer, he said he had to enter his glory. He said the gospel had to be preached in the entire world. Fulfillment of all things positively entailed more than the Cross, thus the Law could not pass at the Cross, because Jesus said all of it had to be fulfilled before any of it could pass.

There is another factor here that is virtually ignored by all those who say that the events of the Cross were all that was necessary for the Law to pass. Was the virgin birth of Jesus, in fulfillment of Isaiah 7:14 necessary before the Law could pass? Was his birth in Bethlehem in fulfillment of the prophecy of Micah 5:2 necessary for the passing of the Law? Was his miraculous ministry foretold by Isaiah 35, absolutely necessary before the Law could pass away?

Now, each of these events was the subject, not of the Law, *per se,* but strictly of "the prophets." If it was essential that these and other events in the life of Jesus had to be fulfilled before the Old Covenant could pass, then that is an admission that "the prophets" had to be fulfilled before the Law could pass. And this means that since Jesus said, "not one jot or one tittle shall pass until all is fulfilled," then you cannot arbitrarily say that only the Law had to be fulfilled, nor can you say that only

33

some prophecy had to be fulfilled. It is illogical to say that it was necessary to fulfill all the prophecies of Jesus' life *before the Cross,* before the Law could pass, but that no Old Covenant prophecies concerning him had to be fulfilled *after the Cross*, for the Law to pass. Jesus said none would pass until all was fulfilled. He did not say all would pass when some was fulfilled.

Finally, if you say the law passed at the Cross, then "heaven and earth" passed at the Cross. Yet Hebrews 12, which positively is speaking about the passing of the Old Law under the imagery of the passing of heaven and earth, *was written after the Cross.* Also, in light of Luke 21:22, it is impossible to say that the Law passed away at the Cross. These are serious objections to the view that the Law fully passed at the Cross.

LAW VERSUS PROPHETS?

The fourth objection offered to negate the force of Matthew 5:17-18 is the claim that what Jesus really meant was that he would fulfill all the legal and moral mandates of the Old Law, and the Old Law would then pass, but he did not really mean all *prophecies* had to be fulfilled. Thus, in this interpretation there is a distinction between the Law and the Prophets.

This interpretation contradicts Luke 24:44. Jesus said, "all things must be fulfilled which were written in the Law of Moses, *and the Prophets and the Psalms* concerning me" (My emphasis). You cannot delineate between *the Law* and the "prophets" in Matthew 5, and then appeal to Luke 24 to prove Jesus fulfilled just *the Law* in his passion. Luke 24 speaks about the law, *the prophets, and the Psalms* and Jesus said *all* had to be fulfilled.

If Jesus was saying he had to fulfill the things written about his death, and if all he had to fulfill was "the Law," as distinct from the prophets, then patently, *the Law of Moses predicted that death*. But, Jesus' death was a matter of *prophecy*, not moral legislation. Where do you find the passion of Christ in the Decalogue? Thus, to appeal to the Cross as the fulfillment of the "Law," and not the "prophets," is self-defeating, *for the Cross was a matter of prophecy*. This raises a very significant issue.

The seventh day Sabbath was an integral, foundational part of "the law." I do not know of anyone that would deny that, since it is embedded in the Decalogue, as the fourth commandment. So, Sabbath was the Law, and Jesus said that all of the Law had to be fulfilled before any of the Law could pass. The question is, how could Jesus fulfill "the Law" i.e. the Sabbath? The fact is, his death alone did not and could not "fulfill," bring into a reality, the meaning of the Sabbath.

Paul says the Sabbaths (all of them) were shadows of good things about to come" (Colossians 2:14-16). What did the Sabbath foreshadow? According to virtually all Jewish and scholarly sources that I will not take the time to document here, the Sabbath foreshadowed final salvation and the resurrection.

There are no futurists who believe that the resurrection of the dead was brought to a reality, fully accomplished at the cross. Let that soak in!

Jesus said not one jot or one tittle of the Law could pass until it was all–every jot and every tittle–fully accomplished. The Law-Sabbath-foreshadowed the final resurrection. Therefore, until the typological, foreshadowing of the Sabbath became a reality, not one jot or one tittle of the Law could pass.

In the Sabbath we have not only a direct mandate, i.e. "Law" but, we likewise have prophecy. To suggest that only one aspect of Sabbath– legal mandate—had to be honored by Jesus, while the prophetic element of the Sabbath remains unfulfilled is surely disingenuous and a violation of Jesus' words.

This means that those who try to delineate between; "the law and the prophets" in Matthew 5 are clearly guilty of a logical fallacy. On the one hand they are saying that Jesus fulfilled the Law, the moral mandates, but *not the prophets*, but, they are saying *that the Cross was the fulfillment of the Law*. However the moral mandates of the Law did not prophesy the Cross. The *prophets* foretold the Cross. Thus, the Cross was a matter of *prophecy*, not law *per se*. And yet, if the Cross was a matter of prophecy, since Jesus said all had to be fulfilled, this means that all prophecy had to be fulfilled before the Old System could pass. The attempt to delineate between the Law and the Prophets is a self-defeating argument. And when you throw the Sabbath into the matrix, the problems of saying the Law passed at the Cross are compounded.

Further, the Law, including the *ceremonial* aspects had a predictive element to it, as we have just suggested in regard to the Sabbath. See Colossians 2:16f. In that passage Paul told the Colossians not to be judged in regard to meat and drink, feast days and Sabbaths. These were all part of the "ceremonial" legislation of the Old Law. But notice, in verse 17 Paul says they all foreshadowed Christ-they were "shadows of good things about to come." Take note of the present active indicative of the text. Those festivals were still, when Paul wrote, shadows of the coming better things, and this is critical.

Please note also that those things were still viewed as *coming*. The Greek text uses the word *mello*, which means, "about to be, to be on the point of." Paul, writing in approximately A.D. 62, said the things of the Old Law were still a shadow of the better things that *were about to come*. He included the Sabbaths in that. Thus, "the Law" and "the Sabbaths" went hand in hand - until final fulfillment.

Jesus said "the law" was *prophetic*. In Matthew 11:13 he said, "For all the prophets and the law prophesied until John." Did you catch that? Jesus said the *Law* and the prophets *prophesied*. This indisputable fact is established by the realization that all of Israel's feast days, her sacrifices, he entire cultus– which of course was patently "the law" were typological and "prophesied" of better things to come. How then can one delineate between the prophets and "the law"? Simply put, he cannot Biblically do so. I suggest that our comments on the Sabbath just above show us how "the Law" could also be prophetic, since Sabbath was "the law" but prophetically anticipated the final resurrection.

In addition, in Hebrews 10:1-4 the writer says the Law was a shadow of good things *about to come,* (once again, just as in Colossians 2, those things were viewed as not yet fully come). The significant things about Hebrews 10:1-4 is that it refers to the Old Covenant High Priestly actions and their symbolic meaning, as *the Law*. The Hebrew writer referred to *the prophetic nature* of the Old Covenant sacrificial and sacerdotal actions as *the Law*. These actions included the return of the High Priest from the Most Holy Place. Jesus said not one jot or one tittle would pass from the Law, until it was all fulfilled. Since *the Law* included the sacrificial and sacerdotal (priestly) actions, including the return of the High Priest from the Most Holy Place, then until Christ returned (returns?) from the Most Holy Place, *the Law* has not been fulfilled, and therefore remains valid.

The point is that Hebrews uses the term *the Law* in direct reference *to the Old Covenant prophetic sacrifices and services* that Jesus had to fulfill in his priestly role. Pay particular attention to the fact that the writer says "the first covenant had ordinances of divine service" (Hebrews 9:1-3). Since the covenant was "the law" and "the law" was the covenant, it is *prima facie* true that the prophetic, typological elements of "the covenant" were in fact "the law." Thus, every jot and every tittle of "the law" which included those typological cultic festivals and sacrifices, was fulfilled.

Those who say that Jesus only had to fulfill *the Law and not the prophets*, are confronted with the reality that Biblically, *the Law* included the prophetic nature of the sacrifices and the actions of the High Priest. But, again, for Jesus to completely fulfill the prophetic nature of those sacrifices and services, he had to come again the second time. The Law would not be completely fulfilled until Christ returned.

Our point is that one cannot delineate between the Law and the Prophets for *the Law itself was prophetic*. Jesus' referent to the Law prophesying almost certainly refers to the typological nature of the sacrificial system, for again, the moral mandates of the Decalogue were not in themselves prophetic or typological. Jesus had to fulfill all the prophetic scriptures whether couched in types, symbols, visions or oracles.

Furthermore, *the prophets are very clearly called the Law.* In I Corinthians 14:21-22, Paul quotes from Isaiah 28, and specifically calls it "the law." A check of Romans 3:10f will reveal that Paul quotes from the Psalms, Jeremiah, Proverbs and Isaiah, and calls all of them *the Law,* (v. 19). In addition, as noted above, *the law prophesied* (Matthew 11:13). Now since the prophets are called "the law," and since "the law" *prophesied,* one cannot delineate between the law and prophets in Matthew 5.

Our point is that the term "the Law" was the abbreviated way of referring to the entire Old Covenant. When Jesus said, "One jot or one tittle will in no wise pass from the Law until all be fulfilled," he was using the form of speech prevalent in his time. He did not need to say, "Law and Prophets" or, "Law, Prophets and Psalms" each and every time.

When Jesus said he did not "come to destroy the Law and the Prophets, but to fulfill," he was saying he came to fulfill all the *Law and prophets.* He was using a form of *ellipsis.* When he said he did not come to destroy the Law and Prophets, but to fulfill, he did not have to say "all the Law and Prophets" again. It was understood that was what he meant. This being true, patently, Jesus did not say that just the Law, to the exclusion of the prophets had to be fulfilled before the Old System could pass. In fact, he did say all the prophets had to be fulfilled before the Old Law could pass.

As we have seen from Romans and Corinthians, inspiration called Jeremiah and Isaiah, in other words *the prophets, the Law.* Jesus said *all of the Law* had to be fulfilled before it could pass, thus, *all of the prophets,* since they were *the Law,* had to be fulfilled before *the Law* could pass. Further, Hebrews called the typological, sacrificial and sacerdotal (priestly) services *the Law* (Hebrews cf. 7:10f; 10:1-2). Jesus said *none of the Law* would pass until it was *all fulfilled.* Therefore, *all* of the typological, sacrificial and sacerdotal services had to be fulfilled before *the Law* could pass.

What we see then is that when one attempts to have Jesus say that all he had to do was fulfill *the law, as opposed to the prophets,* before the Law could pass, he imposes a non-scriptural and artificial distinction upon the term *the Law.* Second, he ignores the elliptical language of Matthew 5:18, and ignores the fact that the Old Law itself, even the legislative edicts, were prophetic in nature. Jesus did indeed have to fulfill all the law and prophets before the Old Law could pass.

FULFILLING THE PROMISES
AND PURPOSE OF THE LAW

Here is a question: If a law or covenant has been abrogated, are any of its penalties or promises applicable anymore? Yes, or No? Will you please get a pencil and circle the one you believe is correct?

Common sense says that if a law is no longer in effect then its penalties or promises are voided. Lamentably, common sense is in short supply when it comes to hanging onto preconceived ideas!

In numerous personal exchanges and even in formal written debates, I have had my opponents actually claim that even after a law or covenant has been annulled, the penalties or promises of that now dead covenant can be applied! I will not "name names" here, but, in one exchange my Amillennial opponent claimed that Covenant sanctions found in the Law of Blessings and Cursings - i.e. national judgment for violating Torah – were brought on Israel in AD 70, even though the Law of Blessings and Cursings was "nailed to the Cross in AD 33." When pressed for either scriptural, logical, or legal precedent or support for this idea, nothing was forthcoming, and the correspondence abruptly ended.

Consider this in light of Jesus' words in Matthew 5:17-18. If the Old Covenant was abrogated at the Cross does this not mean that all Old Covenant promises and penalties were either fulfilled or abrogated at that time? If not, why not? Let's see what this means.

Paul emphatically says his eschatology is taken directly from the Old Covenant (Acts 24:14f; Acts 26:21f). Specifically, the promise of the resurrection was an Old Covenant promise made by Moses and all the prophets. But Paul was speaking about this promise *several years after the Cross=—where, we are told, the Old Covenant was taken away.* But if the Old Covenant was taken away at the Cross how could Paul, years afterward, still be preaching Old Covenant promises? You see, if the Law was nullified at the Cross, *then all of it was nullified.* Remember, Jesus said *none* would pass until *all* was fulfilled. If *all* was not fulfilled, then *none* of it passed! The Old Covenant stands or falls as a *whole*!

The Old Covenant had several constituent prophetic elements and it was essential that they all be fulfilled before the Old Covenant could pass and the New Covenant world be fully established. Among other things, the Old Covenant predicted:

1. The salvation of the remnant of Israel (Isaiah 2-4). Now, the salvation of the remnant only began on Pentecost. It was an on-going, yet unfinished process when Paul wrote Romans. However he said that God's work of saving the remnant would be completed shortly (Romans 9:28). Further, Revelation also depicts the salvation of the remnant (Revelation 7, 14) and that salvation would not be completed until the arrival of the New Creation.

2. The gathering of the Gentiles (Isaiah 49:6f). The gathering of the Gentiles was Paul's personal ministry (Colossians 1:24f). It was given to him, personally, to complete the mystery of God. If the Old Covenant could not pass until all of it was fulfilled, and that included the ministry of Paul to bring in the fullness of the Gentiles (Romans 11:25-27), then the Old Law could not pass until the completion of Paul's ministry.

3. The giving of a New Covenant (Jeremiah 31:29f). How could the Old Covenant pass before the New Covenant was given? Yet, the writer of Hebrews said that the New was in the process of being delivered, and that the Old Covenant was "nigh unto passing" (Hebrews 8:13).

4. The filling up of the measure of Israel's sin leading to their destruction (Isaiah 65:7f; Daniel 9:24). Isaiah said the time was coming when Israel would fill up the measure of her sin and be destroyed. The New Creation would follow. This is a key Old Testament prophecy. Jesus said that Israel would fill up the measure of her sin in his generation, by killing the apostles and prophets that he sent. Thus, the Old Law was not fulfilled, and could not pass until the number of the martyrs was fulfilled. (See Revelation 6:9-11).

5. The coming of the Lord in judgment of the nations (Isaiah 66, Joel 3:1; Zechariah 14). Those who argue that the Old Law passed at the Cross do not seem to understand that the coming of the Lord, the judgment of the nations, and all "last things" elements are from the Old Testament prophets. Jesus said the Old Law could not pass until all of it was fulfilled. If the Law passed at the Cross, then this means that the Lord came then, and the nations were gathered and judged then.

6. The outpouring of the Holy Spirit (Joel 2:28f). Pentecost was clearly after the Cross. Yet, Peter said the events of Pentecost were the fulfillment of Joel 2:28f. How could this be if the entirety of the Old Law was abrogated at the Cross?

7. Finally, consider that in Romans 11:25-28 Paul spoke of the salvation of Israel at the coming of the Lord. While some claim that the coming of the Lord in this text refers to Jesus' Incarnation this is untenable. The prophetic background for Romans 11:25-28 is Isaiah 27:10f; Isaiah 59:17f, and Jeremiah 31, as virtually all scholars agree.

The thing is that Isaiah 27 and Isaiah 59 clearly and undeniably posit the salvation of Israel at the time of the judgment of Israel for shedding innocent blood. So, the salvation of Israel in Romans 11 would fulfill Isaiah 27 and 59. But, the salvation of Israel in Isaiah 27 / 59 would be at the judgment of Israel for shedding innocent blood– not at the Incarnation of Jesus. Jesus posited the judgment of Israel for shedding innocent blood in AD 70 at his coming in judgment. This means that Romans 11 cannot refer to Jesus' first coming, but to his coming in judgment in AD 70. But, notice what this means for the passing of the Law.

Paul explicitly says that the salvation of Israel would be in fulfillment of God's covenant with Israel: "For this (the salvation of Israel at the coming of the Lord) is my covenant with them, when I take away their sin" (Isaiah 59).

Simply and briefly stated, God's covenant with Israel would remain valid until the consummation and fulfillment of that covenant, at the coming of the Lord. This means that God's covenant with Israel was not nailed to the Cross. Romans 11 is *prima facie* proof that Torah did not pass at the Cross.

If the Old Covenant was abrogated at the Cross how could any of these prophecies be valid after the Cross? Quite simply, they could not. Yet, the New Testament writers repeatedly refer to these prophecies *after Pentecost,* and anticipate their fulfillment. *This unequivocally proves the Old Covenant was not abrogated at the Cross.*

This is also demonstrated in another way. In Acts 13:40f Paul preached to the Jews at Antioch. They rejected the gospel, and Paul warned them, "Behold, ye despisers and wonder and perish, for I work a work in your days, a work, which ye shall in no wise believe, though a man declare it unto him." What is the significance of Paul's words? They are taken from Habakkuk 1:5.

In Habakkuk, Judah was about to be destroyed by the Babylonians, for violating the Law of Moses. The sanctions of the Law of Blessings and Cursings (Deuteronomy 28-30) were about to fall on them. And in *Acts 13, years after the Old*

Covenant was supposedly taken away, Paul was threatening Israel with that identical Old Covenant wrath!

National destruction for violating the Covenant was part and parcel of the Law delivered to Israel (Leviticus 26; Deuteronomy 28-30). *But if that covenant was abrogated at the Cross how could Paul still threaten Israel with covenant wrath?*

It is interesting and significant that this principle is recognized— in unguarded moments—even by those who insist that Torah was annulled at the Cross. Amillennialists such as Ed Wharton, former instructor at the Sunset School of Preaching, when arguing against Premillennialists, takes note of the promise of national restoration found in Deuteronomy 30:1-10. Premillennialists commonly appeal to this text for a future restoration of Israel.

Wharton reasons that since the Old Law is abrogated the promise of restoration is nullified as well. He is patently correct. However but he and all futurists who apply Old Covenant eschatological promises to the future are guilty of inconsistency on this point. If Israel cannot be blessed because the Old Covenant has been abrogated, *then Christ cannot return for the same reason. Both promises are Old Covenant promises.*

Furthermore, if Torah had been annulled when Paul spoke in Acts 13, he could not be threatening Israel with the sanctions of the Old Law. Yet, he was undeniably doing precisely that.

Note our argument:

No promise or penalty of a covenant is applicable if that covenant has been abrogated.

But Paul applied Old Covenant penalties to Israel (Acts 13).

Therefore the Old Covenant penalties were still applicable in Acts 13.

Note another argument:

No promise or penalty of a Covenant is applicable if that Covenant has been abrogated.

The promises of the coming of the Lord, judgment of the nations and the resurrection are Old Covenant promises (Isaiah 66; Daniel 12; Joel 3:1f, etc.)

The Old Covenant was abrogated at the Cross - (traditional view of the Old Covenant).

Therefore the promises of the coming of the Lord, the judgment of the nations, and the resurrection, being Old Covenant promises, were abrogated at the Cross.

If there is a single Old Testament prophecy that is unfulfilled then the Old Covenant still stands. If the Old Testament is truly abrogated then the eschatological prophecies of the Old Testament must be fulfilled or nullified.

The view that the Old Law passed at the Cross strips the New Testament scriptures of all eschatology and demands that every promise of "last things" was fulfilled at the Cross. It suggests that God started over on Pentecost with a totally new set of "last things" promises. (This is precisely the "Replacement Theology" view). This is patently false. The New Testament writers constantly affirm that they are simply reiterating the Old Covenant promises (II Peter 3:1, 13; Revelation 10:6f). Their "One Hope" was nothing but the hope of Israel found in

"Moses, the Law and the prophets" (Acts 24:14f). There is no "new" New Testament eschatology.

The Old Covenant promises of the coming of the Lord, judgment and resurrection had to be fulfilled before the New Covenant world of Jesus could be perfected. Those promises of "the end," as seen above, do not deal with the end of time, but with the end of the Old Covenant world of Israel and the full establishment of the New Covenant world of Christ.

The Old Law could not pass until it had accomplished its purpose – this is established in Galatians 3:23-25. Paul says those under the law were "under guard," "kept for the faith which would afterward be revealed." He says the Law was given to serve as a "tutor" (NKJV) to bring them to Christ. He then concludes by saying, "after faith is come we are no longer under a tutor."

Plainly, "the faith" Paul has in mind is not the subjective faith of individuals, but the objective *system of faith,* the Gospel System. The Law was to continue until "The Faith" came. Did "The Faith" come at the Cross? Patently not, although the Cross is where the New Covenant of "The Faith" was confirmed by the death of Jesus the Testament maker (Galatians 3:15).

It is also important to note that Paul speaks of those under the Law as children, heirs, put under the authority of the guardian, until the time appointed by the Father (Galatians 5:1-2). That would be the time of receiving the *inheritance* promised to Abraham. That inheritance could not be achieved under or through the Law (Galatians 3:18f). *The Law was to deliver them to the time for receiving that inheritance promised to Abraham.* So, the key question is: What was the inheritance promised to Abraham? It was the heavenly city and country; it was the better resurrection (Hebrews 11:13-16, *35f), the New Creation*!

So, the Law was to *endure until the inheritance promised to Abraham arrived*. To reiterate, the Law was to serve as the "tutor" or "guardian" until the time for the reception of that inheritance.

Peter said they were still looking for that New Creation when he wrote 2 Peter 3:13f. Furthermore, the writer of Hebrews urged his readers to remain faithful so that they might receive the inheritance promised to Abraham (Hebrews 6:14f; 10:36f). Likewise, John wrote eloquently of the impending reception of that heavenly city and New Creation (Revelation 21-22). Since Torah was to endure until the time of the inheritance, and since that heavenly inheritance had not yet been delivered this proves that the Law was still in effect when these books were written, long after the Cross. This point is very critical.

Let me re-state this critical fact: The Abrahamic promises were the goal of the Old Covenant. While the Old Covenant could not deliver the promises of the new world, redemption and salvation, *it could deliver the Old Covenant Saints to the new world*. Further, the Old Covenant could not pass until it had delivered Israel to that "promised land" of the New Covenant world. That is Paul's point in Galatians.

The Old Covenant predicted the coming of a New Covenant (Jeremiah 31:29f). Did the Old Covenant pass away before that predicted New Covenant was delivered? If so, the Old Covenant passed away *before it had fulfilled its purpose in bringing Israel to a New Covenant*. Conversely, if you say that the Law of Moses has been taken away, you are thereby affirming "Covenant Eschatology" i.e. the fulfillment of all prophecy, including that of the New Creation and the resurrection. As we have seen, Torah was to endure until the reception of the Abrahamic inheritance.

As we have seen, in Hebrews 8:8-13 the writer recalls God's promise given in Jeremiah, and then says, "In that he says 'a

48

new covenant' he has made the first obsolete. Now what is becoming obsolete and growing old is ready to vanish away."

The Hebrew writer was living in the last days of the Old Covenant, when the New Covenant was being delivered (Hebrews 1:1-2). As he writes, he recalls God's promise to give the New Covenant, and says the Old was ready to vanish away. The Old had not yet been fulfilled. It had not yet fulfilled its function because the promised New Covenant was not yet fully delivered. But the writer says the Old was "ready to vanish." "Ready to vanish" does not mean *already* vanished.

The Old Law was in a time of transition. The New Covenant had to be fully given before the full purpose of the Old was completed, and Paul very clearly says the Law was to last until "the Faith" was delivered. Would anyone assert the New Covenant was fully delivered at the Cross? At Pentecost? Surely not. Therefore, until the Law had fulfilled its purpose in bringing Israel to the New Covenant it did not pass away.

Finally, consider the necessity for the "fulfillment of all things" in light of Daniel 9:24, as it relates to Matthew 5:17-18. In this marvelous passage, Daniel was told that six things were determined, "upon your people and your holy city" (v. 24). One of those things was to "finish transgression" which refers to the filling up of the measure of sin. See our comments on Isaiah 65.

Israel did not fill up her sin at the Cross. Jesus said she would fill up her sin by persecuting the "apostles and prophets" that he would send (Luke 11:49). Further, Paul said that in persecuting the apostles, Israel was in fact filling up the measure of her guilt (1 Thessalonians 2:16f). Yet, he wrote this years after the Cross, thus, Daniel 9 was not fulfilled at the Cross.

Another element foretold was that in that pivotal seventy weeks, God would, "make atonement for iniquity." This is a referent to the Cross. However *the Atonement was not finished at the Cross*.

Remember our discussion of Hebrews 9:8f above. Jesus had to fulfill the High Priestly functions to fulfill the Old Covenant. Well, he offered himself as a sacrifice, but the Atonement was not finished then. He entered the Most Holy Place, just as the High Priest did, but the Atonement was not consummated by his entrance into the Most Holy. To complete the Atonement process, *he had to come out of the Most Holy Place*, just as Hebrews says he was about to do very, very soon (Greek *hosan, hosan micron*, Hebrews 10:37). Without this final act, the Atonement was not completed. (Note that in Leviticus 9:22, the blessing of the Atonement was not bestowed until the High Priest came out of the Most Holy Place). Yet, Daniel 9 unequivocally says the seventy weeks were determined for the making of the Atonement.

Daniel was *not* told that the Atonement would be "begun" or initiated, to be consummated millennia later. He was *not* told that there would be a gap of two thousand years between the offering of the sacrifice, entrance into the Most Holy, and then the coming out of the Most Holy. The making of Atonement was confined to the seventy weeks of Daniel. This means, undeniably, that Christ's *parousia*, to fulfill the High Priestly function, had to be at no later than the end of the seventy weeks, and according to Daniel 9, the end of the seventy weeks was the fall of Jerusalem in A.D. 70.

Here is where the inconsistency of the traditional view is exposed. We are told that the Law passed away at the Cross when Jesus "fulfilled all things." *However he did not fulfill all of Daniel 9:24 on the Cross*.

☛ Israel's sin was not filled up at the Cross.

☛ Jesus did not finish the Atonement at the Cross.

☛ Everlasting righteousness was not fully accomplished at the Cross, because Peter was still anticipating the arrival of the New Creation, "Wherein dwells righteousness." Likewise, Paul was still "eagerly looking" for the arrival of that everlasting righteousness in Galatians 5:5.

☛ Jesus did not "seal up vision and prophecy" at the Cross, because to seal up vision and prophecy is a comprehensive term encompassing *all prophecy*.

☛ Daniel's vision undeniably referred to the destruction in A. D. 70. So, Jesus did not fulfill that part of Daniel 9 at the Cross.

So, if a person argues that all that was necessary for the Law to pass was for Jesus to die on the Cross, this means that *only part of Daniel 9 had to be fulfilled.* In other words, although there are six elements foretold in Daniel 9:24, we are asked to believe that when Jesus died, the Law passed away, before all of those elements were fulfilled. This means that when *one part of one part* of Daniel 9:24, i.e. the *sacrifice* of the Atonement process, was fulfilled, *all of the Law* was taken away. *However heaven decreed that all of Daniel 9 had to be fulfilled, and that it would not be fulfilled until the time of the end, the fall of Jerusalem!* If the Old Covenant was removed at the Cross, however, this means that when Jesus died, to *initiate* Atonement, that *the other elements of Daniel 9:24 were nullified*, because at the point of the Cross the entirety of the Old Covenant passed away.

But again, this is not what Jesus said in Matthew 5. He said, "*None* would pass until *all* was fulfilled." Furthermore, Daniel's vision did not say the seventy weeks were determined to accomplish *part* of the six things. Now since the six items encompassed Jesus' ministry, the persecution of the church and the parousia to consummate the Atonement, it is clear that before the Law could pass, the entire spectrum of the events foretold in Daniel had to find fulfillment. (See my book, *Seventy Weeks Are Determined...For the Resurrection*, for a fuller discussion of these issues).

Patently, therefore, to argue that the Law passed away at the Cross ignores the Biblical reality. The Old Law had to fulfill all of its purposes and promises before it could pass. Among those promises was the deliverance of Israel to the reception of the Abrahamic inheritance, which was the New Creation-and the better resurrection. Among those promises was the fulfillment of Daniel 9, which would consummate in the arrival of the New Covenant world of the Messiah at the dissolution of the Old Covenant world of Israel in A.D. 70. The Old Law, the Law of Moses, did not pass until A.D. 70.

The traditional view of the passing of Torah says SOME of the Law would pass when SOME was fulfilled.

Jesus said NONE of Torah would pass until it was ALL Fulfilled.

Isn't there something tragically wrong when, in order to maintain traditional views, we have to totally distort Jesus' words?

It is time to take Jesus seriously and reject the idea that the Law of Moses passed away at the Cross.

Torah could not pass until the reception of the Abrahamic inheritance, the New Creation / Resurrection.

If that inheritance has not arrived, Torah remains valid.

If Torah has passed, all eschatological prophecies have been fulfilled.

There is no other choice.

SUMMARY AND CONCLUSION

What have we seen in this work?

We have seen that "heaven and earth" had to pass away before the Old Law could pass away.

We have shown that this "heaven and earth" was the Old Covenant world of Old Israel.

We have seen that instead of predicting the destruction of physical heaven and earth the Bible predicted the passing of Old Israel's world in order for God to create the new world of His Son – the Kingdom of God – the church of the living God.

We have seen that the Bible clearly tells when ALL prophecy was to be fulfilled – when heaven and earth would pass – in 70 AD with the destruction of the city of Jerusalem, the heart and core of Israel's world.

We have examined several objections, and found them to be based upon false suppositions.

We have seen that if the Old Covenant has been abrogated then all of its prophecies including the predictions of the "end" must be fulfilled or abrogated. If those prophecies have not been fulfilled then the Old Covenant still stands.

We have seen that the Old Law could not pass until it had fulfilled its purpose, and that purpose included deliverance to the New Covenant. That was not fulfilled until the entire New Covenant was revealed and confirmed. That simply did not happen at the Cross – or Pentecost.

We have seen that Daniel 9 precludes the possibility that the Law passed at the Cross. Daniel said all things written would be fulfilled by the time of the fall of Jerusalem (in A.D. 70).

Matthew 5:17-18 says that all things had to be fulfilled for the Old Covenant to pass. Therefore, all of the events of Daniel 9, which extended to A.D. 70, had to be fulfilled before the Law could pass. We have seen that Jesus unequivocally stated that in the fall of Jerusalem "all things that are written" would be fulfilled.

The ideas presented in this work are representative of what is called *Covenant Eschatology*. This is the view that God has kept His promises in fulfilling all prophecy by the time of the passing of Old Israel in 70 AD.

The fall of Jerusalem was far more than the passing of the capital of Judaism – it was a spiritually cosmic, universal event. It was the time of the coming of Jesus (Matthew 24:29-34), the judgment (Matthew 16:27-28). It was at that time that the salvation in Christ was fully revealed (Colossians 3:1f). It is because of what happened then, as the consummation of the work started on the Cross (Hebrews 9:26-28), that you and I can have confidence in the Word of God and the God of the Word. Christ did come in judgment of the old world in A.D. 70, and fully established the unending New Covenant Heaven and Earth. That is when all things foretold by the prophets were fulfilled, and that is how heaven and earth passed away.

CPSIA information can be obtained
at www.ICGtesting.com
Printed in the USA
LVHW03s0003060618
579763LV00007B/176/P